Common Sense HR Solutions

Workplace Harassment Awareness and Prevention
Dealing with Difficult People
Hiring the Right Person for the Right Job
Workforce Diversity and Inclusion

HRCT
Compliance for Success

Common Sense HR Solutions   DavyZ Jones

COMMON SENSE HR SOLUTIONS

Workplace Harassment Awareness and Prevention
Dealing with Difficult People
Hiring the Right Person for the Right Job
Workforce Diversity and Inclusion

© 2018 HRComplianceTraining.Net. All rights reserved.

Except as permitted under the U.S. Copyright Act of 1976, no part of this publication may be reproduced, distributed, or transmitted in any form or by any means, or stored in a database or retrieval system, without the prior written permission of the publisher.

Publisher:

HRComplianceTraining.Net

180 North University Avenue – Suite 270 – Provo, UT 84601

Author

Davy Z. Jones

Second Edition: November, 2018

ISBN - 9781731019899

Common Sense HR Solutions

DavyZ Jones

The author and publisher have made every effort to ensure that the information in this publication was correct at the time of publication. The author and publisher do not assume and hereby disclaim any liability to any party for any loss, damage, or disruption caused by errors or omissions, whether such errors or omissions result from negligence, accident, or any other cause.

DISCLAIMERS – This publication was produced to provide general knowledge about workplace harassment awareness and prevention. Information presented herein is intended to be used for general educational purposes only and should not be construed to be offered in any way as legal advice, counsel, or opinion(s).

NO LEGAL ADVICE OFFERED - Content herein is not intended to convey or constitute legal advice, is not intended to be a solicitation of any kind, and is in no way is a substitution for legal advice obtained from a qualified attorney. We advise you to consult with a qualified employment law attorney for answers to questions relative to your particular situation.

USE OF THIS PUBLICATION - This publication is licensed for your personal use only and may not be re-sold or given away. If you would like to share this publication with colleagues, family, friends, or students, please purchase an additional copy for each person (quantity discounts are available; contact us at info@hrcompliancetraining.net for details).

Written and produced in the United States of America.

Common Sense HR Solutions

DavyZ Jones

Book Contents

Workplace Harassment Awareness and Prevention	7
Dealing with Difficult People	46
Hiring the Right Person for the Right Job	66
If Diversity is the Goal . . . Inclusion is the Means	86
References	104

Common Sense HR Solutions *DavyZ Jones*

This book is dedicated to every employer who believes in enabling employees to freely and fully utilize their abilities and talents to fulfill the organization's mission.

"If a window of opportunity appears, don't pull down the shade." ~ Tom Peters, author of *In Search of Excellence*

Common Sense HR Solutions *DavyZ Jones*

Workplace Harassment

Awareness and Prevention

HRCT
Compliance for Success

Common Sense HR Solutions

DavyZ Jones

Chapter Contents

Workplace Harassment Defined	10
Examples of workplace harassment	13
How Employees Typically React to Workplace Harassment	15
The Business Case for Workplace Harassment Awareness and Prevention Training	17
Proven Strategies to Maintain Awareness of and Prevent Workplace Harassment	21
Select Task Force on the Study of Harassment in the Workplace	24
Bystander Intervention Training	27
Summary	33
Review Questions	37
Answer Key	44

Common Sense HR Solutions

DavyZ Jones

Workplace harassment defined

Workplace harassment defined

Harassment in the workplace is a growing nationwide epidemic that threatens the economic and social stability of millions of employers of all sizes in all industries.

The U.S. Equal Employment Opportunity Commission (EEOC) reports that it received an average of 76 harassment charges every day in 2015, costing employers nearly $165 million in federal court-ordered awards and settlements.

EEOC statistics do not include estimated hundreds of millions of dollars in legal fees, court costs, or judgments and settlements associated with harassment actions adjudicated in local and state courts.

According to a study on workplace conflict commissioned by CPP, Inc., employers in the United States in 2008 gave away approximately $359 billion in lost productivity and employee turnover costs as the result of harassment in the workplace.

Workplace harassment is offensive or unwelcome conduct in any form perpetrated by a colleague, a supervisor, an employer's agent or even a non-employee, Harassment is driven by a reaction to a person's age, ancestry, arrest record, citizenship status, color, gender, genetics, marital status, military status, physical, mental or a perceived disability or handicap, national origin, race, religion, or sexual orientation (including gender identity).

Harassment interferes with a person's ability to perform his or her job or to advance professionally and can be harmful to that person's mental well-being.

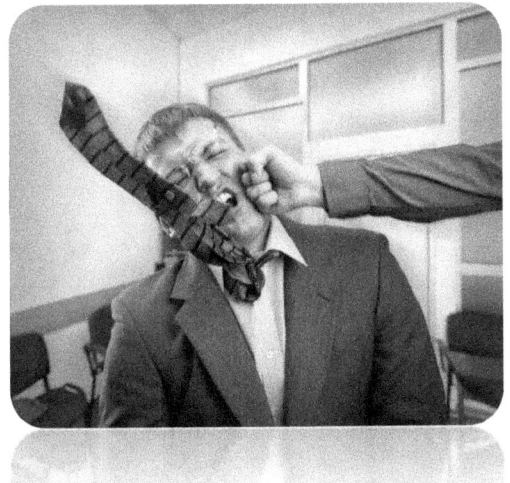

Harassment in action includes but is not limited to epithets, insults, intimidation, mockery, name-calling, offensive jokes, physical assaults, physical threats, presentation of offensive objects or pictures, put-downs, ridicule, slurs, unwanted attention, or unwelcome contact in any form.

Harassment becomes illegal whenever an employee is forced to endure offensive behavior to remain employed and whenever a reasonable person would consider the action to be abusive, hostile, intimidating or inappropriate.

Simple interpersonal annoyances, petty slights, and minor, isolated conflicts do not constitute illegal acts of harassment.

Examples of workplace harassment

Examples of workplace harassment

Workplace harassment comes in various forms from various employees . . . male, female, old, young, experienced, and inexperienced.

Harassment can be physical or verbal and can be committed by any employee, key person, manager, supervisor or even a customer or vendor.

- Co-worker Harassment – Whenever anyone creates a hostile work environment by intimidating, frightening, or making co-workers including employees, customers, or vendors feel uncomfortable, they are guilty of harassment and may be subject to legal action under federal or state anti-harassment laws

- Physical Harassment – Is not as common as verbal harassment but can be more dangerous and even life-threatening and includes grabbing, groping, hitting, kicking, pinching, pushing, sexual contacts, slapping and other forms of inappropriate touching

- Supervisory (quid pro quo) Harassment – Managers, key personnel, and supervisors often use their positions of power to coerce subordinates into agreeing to engage in a variety of illicit activities with offers of job security, pay raises, and promotions

- Verbal Harassment – Is the most common form of workplace harassment and includes innuendos, insults, name-calling, off-color jokes, and threats

Common Sense HR Solutions

DavyZ Jones

How employees typically react to workplace harassment

Common Sense HR Solutions

DavyZ Jones

How employees typically react to workplace harassment

The majority of employers we surveyed in 2015 presume that most employees who experience harassment in the workplace seek redress by filing complaints with the EEOC or by hiring attorneys on their own to file lawsuits in local, state, or federal courts but that presumption is incorrect.

According to a 2016 survey conducted by the EEOC, only about 5% of victims of workplace harassment take legal action. The remaining 95% choose instead to avoid the harasser, downplay or deny instances of harassment or attempt to forget or ignore harassment and rarely even complain about or confront the harasser. That same survey found that only one in three employees who experience workplace harassment even bother to report their experiences to human resources, a manager, supervisor, or union representative.

The business case for workplace harassment awareness and prevention training

Common Sense HR Solutions

Davy2 Jones

The business case for workplace harassment awareness and prevention training

Harassment in any form in your workplace damages your most valuable asset . . . *The women and men who make the organization work* . . . and is therefore ethically and morally wrong on every level, a fact which makes every employer ethically and morally responsible for making every effort to be aware of and prevent any form of workplace harassment.

Moreover, workplace harassment kills profitability. According to the U.S. Equal Employment Opportunity Commission (EEOC), employers lost $164.5 million in 2015 in potential profits paid to employees who were victims of workplace harassment. These losses were in addition to the hundreds of millions of dollars in lost profits paid to harassed employees who prosecuted their cases, without EEOC intervention, in local, state, and federal courts.

The business case for preventing workplace harassment makes economic sense for two reasons:

1. **Direct costs** – includes productivity losses for energy, resources, and time diverted from business operations to confront and assess every act of workplace harassment plus hard cash spent to

hire legal representation, appear for depositions, appear in court, and to pay court-awarded damages, fines, judgments, and settlements. Between 2010 and 2015, employers paid nearly $700 million in compensation to harassed employees through the EEOC's pre-litigation process. These direct costs are in addition to hundreds of millions of dollars in post-trial awards assessed by judges and juries plus countless millions of dollars employers spent on court costs and lost employee time.

2. **Indirect costs** – includes countless millions of dollars in lost productivity, increased employee turnover, and damage to an organization's brand and reputation. Even the mere allegation of workplace harassment can damage an organization's ability to attract new employees and to retain customers or clients or to attract new customers or clients. Productivity can fall off significantly when harassed employees become disheartened and distracted and disengage from job responsibilities, show up late to work or may even stop showing up at all. Workplace harassment stresses not only employees who are direct targets of bullying but also puts pressure on employees who may witness or may be aware of the harassment. When employers 'do the math', they begin to see how minutes, hours, days, weeks, and months of productivity lost to the ramifications of workplace harassment, including blaming, gossiping, retaliation, planning defensive actions, and navigating the resultant drama, all of which can become a severe drag on cash flow and profits.

Common Sense HR Solutions

The bottom line . . . Because any harasser can single-handedly damage employee morale and the economic well-being of any organization, more employers than ever recognize that consistent harassment awareness and prevention training is essential to improving workforce harmony and increasing productivity and profits.

California. Colorado, Connecticut. Delaware, Florida, Massachusetts, Michigan, New York City, New York State, Oklahoma, Rhode Island, Tennessee, Utah, and Vermont require or 'encourage' employers to protect themselves and their employees by providing regularly scheduled workforce harassment training.

The Supreme Court has said that harassment training and anti-harassment policies can be used as an affirmative defense if and when an employer is on trial for workplace harassment.

*Proven strategies to maintain
awareness of and prevent workplace harassment*

Common Sense HR Solutions

DavyZ Jones

Proven strategies to maintain awareness of and prevent workplace harassment

Senior management commitment - Effectively eliminating the threat of harassment in the workplace is possible only when business owners and senior managers are intractably committed to investing in, promoting, and maintaining a diverse, inclusive, respectful, and harmonious workplace in which any form of discrimination or harassment is just not tolerated.

Survey employees - A first step in communicating the organization's commitment to a harassment-free workplace is to survey employees to determine whether harassment currently exists and to measure the potential for future incidents of harassment. Survey results should be shared with all employees and an open discussion of policies and procedures to remedy any existing or potential problems should ensue.

Develop viable anti-harassment policies and procedures - The next step would be to craft sensible, appropriate anti-harassment policies and procedures, supplemented by objective, relevant training to ensure that all employees understand how to utilize those policies and procedures so they can be constantly aware of, prevent, and accurately report workplace harassment incidents. It is critical to establish a reporting system by which employees who've experienced harassment and employees who observe harassment can accurately and confidentially report to designated members of management. Anti-harassment policies should include ironclad guarantees against retaliation in any form. For this step to fully succeed, senior management must be willing to give key personnel the authority and power to ensure company-wide compliance with all anti-harassment policies and procedures.

Equal, proportionate, discipline for any harassers - Any organization that seriously expects to eradicate workplace harassment must be willing to hold any employees accountable, appropriately and meaningfully, for any incidents of harassment. Whenever incidents of workplace harassment are discovered, discipline should be immediate and proportioned to the severity of the event and applied equally to all employees, including 'long-timers,' key personnel, and senior managers.

Implement viable 'zero tolerance' anti-harassment policies and procedures - While leadership and accountability establish the foundation for an employer's anti-harassment culture, viable 'zero tolerance' policies and procedures build the framework to protect employees, clients, and vendors from the threat of workplace harassment.

Invest in reality-based employment law training - Last but not least, the organization's leadership must be willing to invest the money and time necessary to procure easily accessible, made-to-order, timely harassment awareness and prevention training for all employees, including key personnel, senior managers, and owners and partners.

Common Sense HR Solutions

DavyZ Jones

Select Task Force
on the Study of Harassment in the Workplace

Select Task Force on the Study of Harassment in the Workplace

A 2016 report issued by the *Select Task Force on the Study of Harassment in the Workplace* said, "We believe effective training can reduce workplace harassment, and recognize that ineffective training can be unhelpful or even counterproductive. However, even effective training cannot occur in a vacuum - it must be part of a holistic culture of non-harassment that starts at the top. Similarly, one size does *not* fit all: Training is most effective when tailored to the specific workforce and workplace, and to different cohorts of employees. Finally, when trained correctly, middle-managers and first-line supervisors, in particular, can be an employer's most valuable resource in preventing and stopping the harassment."

The Select Task Force study goes on to say, "New and Different Approaches to Training Should Be Explored. We heard of several new models of training that may show promise for harassment training. 'Bystander intervention training' - increasingly used to combat sexual violence on school campuses - empowers co-workers and gives them the tools to intervene when they witness harassing behavior and may show promise for harassment prevention."

The study concludes, "Harassment in the workplace will not stop on its own - it's on all of us to be part of the fight to stop workplace harassment. We cannot be complacent bystanders and expect our workplace cultures to change themselves. For this reason, we suggest exploring the launch of an *It's on Us* campaign for the workplace. Originally developed to reduce sexual violence in educational settings, the *It's on Us* campaign is premised on the idea that students, faculty, and campus staff should be empowered to be part of the solution to sexual assault, and should be provided the tools and resources to prevent sexual assault as engaged bystanders. Launching a similar *It's on Us* campaign in workplaces across the nation - large and small, urban and rural - is an audacious goal. But doing so could transform the problem of workplace harassment from being about targets, harassers, and legal compliance, into one in which co-workers, managers, supervisors, clients, customers, suppliers, and vendors all have roles to play in stopping such harassment."

Bystander intervention training

Common Sense HR Solutions

Bystander intervention training

In the fall of 2009, a dozen bystanders stood by and, without so much as a word of protest, watched as a teenage girl was assaulted outside a California high school. While many of the bystanders had cell phones and some even recorded the attack, no one intervened to stop the assault. Experts define this type of fecklessness as 'bystander inaction.'

Bystander inaction often results from a phenomenon known as 'bystander effect' . . . A circumstance caused by the fact that bystanders are not likely to make an effort to intervene unless and until at least one person takes action.

Bystander intervention training teaches employees why, when, and how to take responsibility for ensuring the safety of their colleagues in the workplace by intervening whenever they witness any form of harassment. This training is designed to change passive bystanders into active bystanders who are capable of effectively discouraging, preventing, and interrupting acts of harassment.

Bystander intervention training helps eradicate workplace harassment by:

1. Changing your workforce's perception of what is and what is not acceptable behavior
2. Eliminating a harasser's ability to shift blame to his or her victim
3. Making workplace harassment a community problem requiring a community solution
4. Turning bystanders into allies who can use peer pressure to protect harassment victims

Bystander intervention works when your employees have been trained to:

1. Be constantly aware of the potential for anyone in or around the workplace to harass another person or persons
2. Recognize when an act of harassment is occurring
3. Determine whether it will be more useful to intervene or to report a potential act of bullying or an in-process act of harassment
4. Know why, how, and when to intervene appropriately, safely, and successfully to diffuse the potential for any form of harassment to continue

Who is a bystander?

You're a bystander when you witness a harassing incident and are not directly involved. As a bystander, you have a choice to make: you can do nothing, or you can calmly and safely intervene by discouraging, interrupting, or preventing an incident.

Common Sense HR Solutions

What does workplace harassment look like to a bystander?

You'll recognize a harasser by the following behaviors, including but not limited to:

- Blocking a person's ability to move from one spot to another
- Displaying or sending offensive or suggestive computer-Emails, images, voicemails, or websites
- Making derogatory, offensive, or stereotypical remarks about a person's age, disability, ethnicity, gender, national origin, race, religion, or sexuality
- Making offensive or suggestive gestures
- Staring at another person with a hostile or sexually suggestive expression
- Indecent, unwanted physical contact
- Telling demeaning or evocative jokes or stories
- Any other behavior that disrupts or threatens the sense of safety and security of any individual or individuals in the workplace

How you can avoid becoming a harasser

While we don't have space here to include every possible scenario, we ask that you ask the following questions about any behavior that might be considered to be harassment. If you are ever tempted to harass anyone in the workplace, you should ask if you would do or say something distressing;

- In front of your parents, partner, or spouse?
- To your minister, priest, or rabbi?

- To a person of your ethnicity, gender, race, or religion?

Or you can ask . . .

- Would I want to be on the wrong end of my harassing words or acts?
- Would I harass a member of my family or a friend with my inappropriate actions or words?

Okay . . . we've defined the problem . . . so; we'll tell you that the best solution is to change the culture in your workplace to make any forms of harassment by anyone at any time completely unacceptable.

When is bystander intervention appropriate?

Bystander intervention is appropriate when you are proficient in the skills necessary to safely and effectively prevent potential harassment or put a stop to an in-process act of bullying.

For example, let's assume that you haven't been trained and let's also say that you're at your desk or workstation doing what you do so well when you hear or see person **A** physically, verbally, or sexually harass person **B**.

What could you do, what would you do? Would you ignore the harassment or would you attempt to put an end to it?

While you might want to get physical with the harasser, that would be your worst possible choice for a couple of reasons: 1. Your act of violence could result in the harasser retaliating by physically attacking you and the victim or, 2. You could put yourself in a position of being arrested, hauled away, and prosecuted for felony assault.

A more effective response might be for you to speak up for the victim by making eye contact with the harasser and saying something like:

- "Do you want me to call for a supervisor?"
- "Knock it off . . . I don't want to call for a supervisor but I will."
- "Please stop . . . we're not here to harass each other; we're here to work."
- "We don't tolerate any form of harassment here."

Or, you might enlist the help of others by:

- Asking a colleague to help you intervene
- Taking advantage of strength in numbers by convincing co-workers to join you in approaching the harasser to ask him or her to stop

The bottom line

Your willingness to intervene as an innocent bystander will help others to understand that harassment is not acceptable in your workplace and that understanding could be the most powerful tool you'll ever use to help eliminate harassment in your workplace . . . once and for all.

Note: Never hesitate to call 911 if you are ever concerned about a harasser's potential to harm you or anyone else in the workplace

Summary

Common Sense HR Solutions

DavyZ Jones

Summary

The ever-changing economy, including the recovery from the 2008 crash and coping with political uncertainties coupled with globalization, has put America's employers and employees under incredible economic pressure. For better or for worse, our economic transformation has led to significant increases in claims of workplace harassment.

While each harassment claim represents a threat to workplace harmony, productivity, and, ultimately, profitability, an employer can take sensible steps to not only minimize those threats but can also use anti-harassment policies and procedures to help create and sustain a harmonious, productive, profitable workforce.

The following guidelines can help prevent workplace harassment claims and reduce the corresponding drain on profits:

1. **A top-down commitment to eliminate workplace harassment** – Owners, senior managers, and key personnel must publicly make personal commitments to promoting civility and respect along with zero tolerance policies and procedures against workplace

harassment, thereby discouraging employees from engaging in any form of harassing conduct

2. **A transparent, concise, confidential reporting process** – The process should guarantee that any employee who is a victim of workplace harassment or is aware of workplace harassment will not suffer retaliation by colleagues, supervisors, or any other person. To give employees a meaningful level of confidence, it might be helpful if employers implemented an independent third-party hotline they could use to report incidents of workplace harassment confidentially

3. **No retaliation** – An employer's anti-harassment policy should guarantee that every report of workplace harassment will be handled with complete confidentiality and the employer should agree in writing to protect every person who reports any form of harassment from any act of retaliation

4. **Regularly scheduled Anti-harassment training** – The essential part of a viable anti-harassment program is regularly scheduled harassment awareness and prevention training for HR professionals, managers, key personnel, and all other employees. Harassment Awareness and Prevention Training can be conducted by human resources professionals or by employment law attorneys. Every HR trainer should be willing to meet with any employer before any scheduled training sessions to ensure that training content and presentation will adequately address the specific needs of each employer.

We join the EEOC and states like California in recommending that

Common Sense HR Solutions

DavyZ Jones

supervisors and employees receive periodic training on how to implement proven workplace harassment awareness and prevention strategies and tactics.

For a no-cost, no-obligation consultation on how you can improve productivity with cost-effective, made-to-order workplace harassment training, contact us at 877-763-2752 or send an Email to admin@hrcompliancetraining.net.

Review questions

Review questions

1. Which of the following would be considered by the Equal Employment Opportunity Commission (EEOC) not to be workplace harassment?

   a) One of your colleagues has an arrest record and when that information becomes general knowledge; another colleague begins to badger him, referring to him as a 'jailbird'

   b) A customer approaches your will-call counter and verbally threatens your colleagues because his order isn't ready for pickup

   c) A supervisor is concerned about an employee's ability to adequately perform her duties as described in her job description and pulls her aside to talk in private about how she can improve on-the-job performance

   d) An unmarried colleague is expecting a child. A supervisor whose attitudes about marriage and childbearing were formed in the 1950s feels offended and publicly questions the lady's morality

   e) Two long-term employees are frustrated by having to work side-by-side in a confined workspace and often fuss over petty conflicts like an old married couple

2. According to a 2016 survey conducted by the EEOC, 95% of harassment victims "choose to avoid the harasser, downplay or deny instances of harassment or attempt to forget or ignore

harassment and rarely even complain about or confront the harasser. Using reason and logic, why, in your opinion, would so many victims refuse to take a public stand against workplace harassment? Is it because they:

a) Are not trained to understand their rights under the law and don't know how to respond to a harasser effectively or how to safely contact management?

b) Believe that workplace harassment is no big deal . . . thinking, "If it doesn't bother management or my colleagues enough to do anything to prevent it, why should I make a federal case out of workplace harassment?"

c) Fear retaliation by management and co-workers?

d) Feel like harassment merely is part of the workplace culture so it wouldn't do any good to 'rock the boat'?

e) All of the above

3. The EEOC reports that in 2015 federal courts ordered employers to pay $164.5 million in damages, fines, judgments, and settlements for workplace harassment claims. Additional direct and indirect employer costs for workplace harassment claims include:

a) Awards, penalties, judgments, and settlements ordered by local and state courts

b) Direct payments to 'fixers' who manage to convince harassment victims to drop their claims

c) Increased employee turnover and difficulties in recruiting new employees

d) Legal fees, court costs, and time lost by employees, managers, supervisors, and company owners

e) Loss of revenues from customers and clients put off by an employer's reputation for enabling workplace harassment

f) Productivity losses due to distractions, interruptions, and loss of morale caused by workplace harassers

g) All of the above

4. **Proven strategies to maintain awareness of and prevent workplace harassment include:**

   a) A commitment on the part of senior management to consistently promote and maintain a harassment-free workplace

   b) Developing an employee handbook that suggests ways to get along on the job

   c) Employer willingness to hold any individuals responsible for any incidents of harassment

   d) Implementation of 'zero tolerance' anti-harassment policies and procedures

   e) Regularly scheduled anti-harassment training designed to help employees change a workplace culture that tolerates harassment

f) All of the above

5. The 2016 Select Task Force on the Study of Harassment in the Workplace made several recommendations to help "minimize or even eliminate the negative effects of workplace harassment on employee morale, productivity, turnover, and profitability," including:

   a) Employees should avoid reporting harassment to avoid retaliation

   b) Employees, managers, supervisors, clients, customers, suppliers, and vendors should be encouraged to become part of a holistic effort to eliminate workplace harassment

   c) Employers and employees should work together to "transform the problem of workplace harassment from being about targets, harassers, and legal compliance, into one in which co-workers, supervisors, clients, and customers all have roles to play in stopping such harassment."

   d) Middle managers and first line supervisors should recognize that they are critical in the day-to-day effort to help all employees be aware of and take appropriate steps to prevent and report workplace harassment

   e) Training is most effective when it supports an organization-wide no-harassment culture

   f) Training should be tailored to meet the unique needs of a specific workforce and varying employee cultures

g) All of the above

6. Bystander intervention training helps employees learn why, when, and how to safely intervene to eradicate workplace harassment by:

    a) Challenging any harasser to a fist fight to let him or her know who's in charge

    b) Changing your workforce's perception of what is and what is not acceptable behavior

    c) Eliminating a harasser's ability to blame his or her victim

    d) Making workplace harassment a community problem requiring a community solution

    e) Turning bystanders into allies who can use peer pressure to protect victims of harassment

    f) All of the above

7. Bystander intervention is appropriate only when you have the skills necessary to safely and effectively help prevent or stop an act of harassment by doing or saying something like:

    a) Expressing your disapproval by frowning or by shaking your head

    b) Harassing the harasser

    c) Taking advantage of strength in numbers by convincing a colleague to join you in approaching the harasser to ask him or her to stop

d) "I'm going to call for a supervisor."

e) "Knock it off . . . I don't want to call for a supervisor but I will."

f) "Please stop . . . we're not here to harass each other; we're here to work."

g) "We don't tolerate any form of harassment here."

h) All of the above

Common Sense HR Solutions

Answer key to review questions

Common Sense HR Solutions

Answer key to review questions

We want you to get the most out of this book, so we've created this Answer Key to help you evaluate everything you've learned in a matter of minutes, anywhere, anytime.

Thanks for learning with us.

1. Which of the following would be considered by the Equal Employment Opportunity Commission (EEOC) not to be workplace harassment?

    The correct answer: c - A supervisor is concerned about an employee's ability to adequately perform her duties as described in her job description and pulls her aside to talk in private about ways she can improve on-the-job performance

2. According to a 2016 survey conducted by the EEOC, 95% of harassment victims "choose to avoid the harasser, downplay or deny instances of harassment or attempt to forget or ignore harassment and rarely even complain about or confront the harasser." Why, in your opinion, would so many victims refuse to take a public stand against workplace harassment? Is it because they:

    The correct answer: e – All of the above

3. The EEOC reports that in 2015 federal courts ordered employers to pay $164.5 million in damages, fines, judgments, and settlements for workplace harassment claims. Additional direct and indirect employer costs for workplace harassment claims include:

Common Sense HR Solutions

DavyZ Jones

Correct answers: a - Awards fines, judgments, and settlements ordered by local and state courts

c - Increased employee turnover and difficulties in recruiting new employees

d - Legal fees, court costs, and time lost by employees, managers, supervisors, and company owners

e - Loss of revenues from customers and clients put off by an employer's reputation for enabling workplace harassment

f -Productivity losses due to distractions, interruptions, and loss of morale caused by workplace harassers

4. **Proven strategies to maintain awareness of and prevent workplace harassment include:**

    The correct answer: **f** – All of the above

5. **The 2016 Select Task Force on the Study of Harassment in the Workplace made several recommendations to help "minimize or even eliminate the negative effects of workplace harassment on employee morale, productivity, turnover, and profitability," including:**

    Correct answers: b - Employees, managers, supervisors, clients, customers, suppliers, and vendors should be encouraged to become part of a holistic effort to eliminate workplace harassment

    c - Employers and employees should work together to "transform the problem of workplace harassment from being about targets, harassers, and legal compliance, into one in which co-workers, supervisors, clients, and customers all have roles to play in stopping such harassment

d - Middle managers and first line supervisors should recognize that they are critical in the day-to-day effort to help all employees be aware of and take appropriate steps to prevent and report workplace harassment

e - Training is most effective when it supports an organization-wide no-harassment culture

f - Training should be tailored to meet the unique needs of a specific workforce and varying employee cultures

6. **Bystander intervention training helps employees learn why, when, and how to safely intervene to eliminate workplace harassment by:**

    Correct answers: b - Changing your workforce's perception of what is and what is not acceptable behavior

    c - Removing a harasser's ability to blame his or her victim

    d - Making workplace harassment a community problem requiring a community solution

    e - Turning bystanders into allies who can use peer pressure to protect victims of harassment

7. **Bystander intervention is appropriate only when you have the skills necessary to safely and effectively help prevent or stop an act of harassment by doing or saying something like:**

Correct answers: a – Expressing your disapproval by frowning or by shaking your head

c - Taking advantage of strength in numbers by convincing a colleague to join you in approaching the harasser to ask him or her to stop

d - "I'm going to call for a supervisor."

e - "Knock it off . . . I don't want to call for a supervisor but I will."

f - "Please stop . . . we're not here to harass each other; we're here to work."

g - "We don't tolerate any form of harassment here."

Common Sense HR Solutions *DavyZ Jones*

Dealing with difficult people

"Any fool can criticize, condemn,
and complain - and most fools do"

~ Dale Carnegie

Common Sense HR Solutions

DavyZ Jones

Chapter Contents

Doris throws a tantrum	52
Conflict in the workplace is inevitable	55
Conflict does not have to rule your workplace	58
Conflict in the workplace can be positive	60
Proven strategies to deal with difficult people in the workplace	63
Points to ponder	67

Common Sense HR Solutions *DavyZ Jones*

Doris Throws a Tantrum

Common Sense HR Solutions — Davy2 Jones

Doris Throws a Tantrum

It's a cold, grey Monday morning, the last day of the month, when Doris, a highly successful account executive who outsells her nearest colleague by two to one burst into the office shared by three accountants; Jeanne, Marilyn, and Patty.

Without so much as a 'good morning' or 'hello,' Doris barks, "Where's the Palmer file? The client wants the audit finished today . . . who's got the file?"

Patty gives Doris the glare of a *Prius* driver who's just been cut off by a Ferrari in freeway traffic but softly speaks as she says, "It's month-end, Doris, so we're running a little behind . . . please give me a minute, and I'll pull it up for you."

Jeanne and Marilyn keep their eyes glued to their computer screens and continue to tap data into their keyboards, doing their best to pretend that Doris hasn't gone off on another tantrum.

But before Doris can even take a moment to think about coming up with an appropriate response, a rush of panic sets in, her blood pressure increases, and her face turns beet red.

Doris steps up to Patty, gets in her face, and screams, "It's my account! Get me the Palmer file now, or there'll be holy heck to pay!"

You're in the office next door, so you can't help but hear Doris' latest outburst. You manage the accounting department . . . what do you do?

Epilogue: Doris throws a tantrum

Over time, every manager, lead person, supervisor, or another key person in any organization will inevitably have to 'deal' with one or more 'difficult' employees like Doris.

And, as a manager, you don't have the luxury of merely ignoring disruptive behaviors in the workplace. You're obligated to take action to stop the immediate disruptive behavior while ensuring that all employees understand and comply with HR policies designed to monitor and maintain a harmonious, productive working environment for all.

Doris and her direct supervisor need to have a face-to-face meeting to make sure that she understands the organization's anti-harassment policies and to give the supervisor the opportunity to advise Doris that her next tantrum will likely be her last tantrum.

Conflict in the workplace is inevitable

Common Sense HR Solutions — Davy2 Jones

Conflict in the workplace is Inevitable

Conflict between human beings is as old as time itself. From the purported confrontation between Cain and Abel thousands of years ago to the complicated relationships between sophisticated, technologically-oriented women and men who work together today, conflict is as alive and well as ever.

Conflicts in the workplace invariably come up during activities to advance the mission of every employing organization.

Some studies indicate that the typical manager in a contemporary workplace can devote nearly half of her time in any given workday to confronting and resolving some form of interpersonal conflict.

If a manager is unable to remain constantly aware of the potential for conflict and effectively prevent conflict, he or she is not only risking the organization's ability to be productive and profitable, the manager can ultimately wind up on the wrong side of a lawsuit and become personally liable for damages awarded by a judge or jury.

It's no secret that any time a disruptive employee like a Doris in our opening example is allowed to be rude, complain, gossip, harass, ignore directives, shout, or shun others, everyone's ability to perform their jobs will be impacted negatively.

So, we understand and agree that conflict in the workplace is inevitable; you've experienced it, and I've experienced it . . . the question that begs to be answered is what can be done to minimize it?

Conflict does not have to rule in your workplace

Common Sense HR Solutions

DavyZ Jones

Conflict does not have to rule in your workplace

The foundation of every successful organization rests on the respect and trust of its workforce; each employee, therefore, has a responsibility to communicate with management and colleagues with complete, consistent professionalism.

If your organization sets clear boundaries on interpersonal behaviors and

relationships, provides consistent training to motivate employees to embrace organizational values, and if you encourage open communications, you'll be well on your way to eliminating the negative consequences of workplace conflict.

Every employee should be thoroughly trained on what is and what is not acceptable behavior and should also be empowered to let any colleague, including key personnel, managers, supervisors and even partners and owners, know when their behavior crosses the line.

Conflict in the workplace can be positive

Common Sense HR Solutions

DavyZ Jones

Conflict in the workplace can be positive

Let's face it . . . when anyone mentions conflict in the workplace, words like anger, hurt feelings, resentment, stress, tension, and perhaps even physical confrontations come to mind.

But conflict, adequately motivated and managed, can be constructive; it can be the fuel that drives an organization to become more creative, more effective, more efficient, more exciting, and, hopefully, more profitable.

If Joe Johnson who manages the billing department is frustrated because there are too many unnecessary steps in the billing process (in his considered opinion) and he goes to the CFO and suggests a better, more efficient way to bill clients that allows the organization to collect money more quickly . . . there is the likelihood of conflict.

Why? The CFO may well be embarrassed because she failed to fulfill her responsibility by coming up with Joe's idea before he did.

From Joe's perspective, he's taking a risk by daring to suggest that his boss, the CFO, either didn't see the problem or didn't think it was worth solving.

But who cares?

Joe cares because he doesn't know for sure that his suggestion could cost him his job and the CFO cares because, no matter what choice she makes, her reputation could take a hit.

And, now, we have negative conflict, unless . . . Joe and the CFO see the conflict as a potential positive for both of them because improved billing practices will make the organization financially stronger.

So, what can Joe and the CFO do?

They can recognize that conflict can be a tool they can use to identify, analyze, and find a viable solution for a heretofore unrecognized problem.

Then, they can put their egos aside (egos, by the way, are one of the biggest drivers of conflict in any workplace), and use conflicting ideas to come up with a solution that works for them as individuals and, moreover, improves the overall economic health of the organization.

The downside in this or any conflict scenario can be frightening because if employees, managers, supervisors, and key personnel are unable to see conflict as a potentially positive force for good, the organization may well stagnate and die.

Don't believe it?

Talk to a senior manager at Sears and then talk to a senior manager at Amazon and decide for yourself how they feel about the potential for conflict to be a positive force in the workplace.

Common Sense HR Solutions

DavyZ Jones

Proven strategies to deal with difficult people

Common Sense HR Solutions

DavyZ Jones

Proven strategies to deal with difficult people

Whether you're an employee, a key person, a manager, a supervisor, or a partner or owner, your organization's most important asset is people . . . people who come from differing backgrounds and different cultures and who have varying experiences, education, and even lug around some potentially harmful baggage which means that any or many of them can be, on some level, difficult.

Welcome to America's work world in the 21st century.

No matter what your job responsibilities may be, you have an obligation to yourself, to your colleagues, and to your organization to help difficult people find ways to fit into your workplace.

How can you do that? How can you help some poor soul who may be a jerk or just socially inept fit in, join the team, and make a viable contribution?

You start by watching for conflict . . . more out of the corner of your eye than full-on scrutinizing everyone for any hint of trouble.

Whenever you hear a complaint about harassment in your workplace, make sure that a supervisor engages the harasser and the person or persons harassed in conversations to verify circumstances before you initiate a formal complaint.

Observe how the troublemaker's colleagues are reacting and look for behaviors that can help you determine whether a troublemaker has a severe personality problem, is just a jerk, or is a pretend tough guy who will turn and run if someone stands up for what is right. Try to determine if the troublemaker is ordinarily cooperative, might have a penchant for violence, or may just be having a bad day?

If the problematic employee is worth keeping, you'll have to develop a plan to help the employee get along in the workplace.

The first step is to take the troublemaker aside where the two of you can have a confidential conversation and politely ask what is causing the disruptive behavior. Then stop talking and listen with the intent to understand. Don't step down to the problematic employee's level by arguing, debating, or raising your voice; you'll only make matters worse. Stay calm and focus on the whys and wherefores of harassing or disruptive behaviors so you can help the employee calm down and diffuse the current conflict.

The next step is to determine whether an individual coaching plan will be helpful. Can the difficult employee turn to someone they trust (might even be you) in the workplace to talk about conflict-triggers that cause disruptions that interfere with colleagues who are trying to do their jobs?

If individual coaching isn't the solution, you might want to refer the person to a counselor to help identify and manage the triggers that cause disruptive behavior

Help the difficult person understand that while you are doing your best to understand what drives his or her disruptive behavior, there is a limit to the organization's ability to tolerate further outbursts.

Last but not least, make sure that the disruptive employee knows that the responsibility to work peacefully with colleagues, customers, and vendors is theirs and theirs alone.

As you close out this conversation, remind the person that termination is always an option.

Points to ponder

Points to ponder

- **Make your employment handbook work for all** - Publish a clear, concise no-tolerance anti-harassment policy in an employee handbook to be distributed to everyone in the organization. Your policy should define all aspects of all forms of harassment and should list consequences harassers will face, including suspension or termination. Establish a reporting procedure that includes a toll-free phone number to allow employees to file complaints. Your policy should assure employees that every claim will be taken seriously, will be held in complete confidence, and will protect them from retaliation.

- **Onsite HR training** – There is no more cost-effective way to educate and motivate employees and managers to create and sustain a harmonious, productive, and profitable workplace than by regularly scheduling HR training designed to address your organization's specific cultural and logistical needs.

- **Listen to employees and managers** – Employees are your most valuable asset so you will want to engage them in regular two-way conversations so you can learn how they feel about their jobs, their colleagues, and their futures. Don't 'meet' with employees and managers and don't talk to them. Put your ego aside, ask open-ended questions, and listen to employees and managers and you'll be able to work together to eliminate workplace harassment.

Common Sense HR Solutions　　　*Davy2 Jones*

Hiring the right person

for the right job

"Hire people who are better than you are, then leave them to get on with it. Look for people who will aim for the remarkable, who will not settle for the routine." ~ David Ogilvy, Advertising mogul

Common Sense HR Solutions

DavyZ Jones

Chapter Contents

Hiring the right person defined — 72

Unique hiring challenges in today's labor market — 75

Finding, hiring, and onboarding the right person in the right job is never easy — 78

The interview – the end all and be all of the hiring process — 84

Hiring the right person defined

Hiring the right person defined

"Employees are a company's greatest asset - they're your competitive advantage. You want to attract and retain the best; provide them with encouragement, stimulus, and make them feel that they are an integral part of the company's mission." ~ Anne M. Mulcahy, former CEO, Xerox Corporation

How can you argue with that?

As Anne Mulcahy and so many other notable business leaders like Henry Ford, Lee Iacocca, Michael Dell, and Bill Gates have proven, the single most important thing any organization can do is hire the right person for the right job, presumably at the right time.

Hiring the right person for the right job means that you hire a candidate who is not only technically capable of performing all job-related tasks but will also fit in with and augment your organization's culture.

After all, while technological advances continue to transform how business is conducted in private and public sectors, it's the creativity, dedication, and hard work of human beings that design, produce, and deliver the products and services that make the world go around.

Hiring the right person requires you to implement an intuitive, thoughtful hiring process purposefully designed to attract the best people (not necessarily the best qualified), evaluates each candidate appropriately for the right position, and help each decision-maker in your organization make an informed decision to offer the right job to the right person.

When you hire the wrong person, you usually wind up wasting copious amounts of time and money backtracking while you try to figure out how to make a better choice the next time around.

Every HR professional understands how time-consuming, costly, and demoralizing it can be when an organization recruits, selects, hires, trains, and then must replace an employee who should never have been hired in the first place.

Apply the simple steps outlined herein to match the right candidate to meet your organization's challenges and fit into your unique culture, and you won't have to worry about making another 'bad' hire.

Unique hiring challenges in today's labor market

Common Sense HR Solutions —   *Davy2 Jones*

Unique hiring challenges in today's labor market

There are two unique challenges HR managers must contend with in today's labor market.

First . . . the unemployment rate has dropped to historic lows, and while that is good news for the economy, it can be bad news for HR because it means that many qualified candidates for just about any open position, especially high-tech or key jobs, are very likely already employed.

Secondly . . . according to a 2010 Pew Research report, approximately 10,000 'baby boomers' (the generation of Americans born between 1944 and 1964) are retiring every day and will continue to retire at that rate until 2029.

The loss of boomers has a profound impact on the workplace because it can mean that the work ethics of the available candidates may not be what you expect or need.

Boomers, after all, learned their work ethics (to be on-time, motivated, loyal, and ready-to-work today, tomorrow, and every day) from their parents . . . men and women who, in their teens and twenties, saved the world from being overrun by the likes of Adolph Hitler, Hideki Tojo, and Benito Mussolini by virtue of their work ethic . . . their willingness to work as hard and as long as it took to achieve a common goal.

A strong work ethic is a set of moral principles . . . discipline, desire to produce a quality product or service, integrity, personal responsibility for a job well done, and a sincere appreciation of the importance of working on a team.

While these are the ethics (principles) every employer wants to see in every job candidate, the astounding rate of boomers who are leaving the job market every day makes it that much harder for you to recruit the right person for the right job.

*Finding, hiring, and onboarding
the right person in the right job is never easy*

Common Sense HR Solutions — Davy2 Jones

*Finding, hiring, and onboarding
the right person in the right job is never easy*

It does no good to acknowledge challenges like a declining pool of available candidates unless you also recognize solutions.

And there are workable solutions to the challenges posed by the low unemployment rate and the exodus of boomers from the job market.

First and foremost, everyone in your HR department must understand and accept today's job market for what it is and for what it is likely to become given the globalization of all economies.

To attract the best candidate for an open position, you'll have to do something you may not be accustomed to doing . . . you'll have to find ways to market your organization and the open position to attract the right candidates.

In other words, you'll have to learn how to convince talented candidates that a position with you will be challenging and stimulating and will provide opportunities for meaningful career advancement.

The following strategies will help you open the door to meaningful communication with prospective candidates.

The natural place to start these days is to leverage social media like Facebook and LinkedIn to announce an open position and, over time, begin meaningful conversations with prospective applicants.

You'll also want to make sure that your website design and content is appealing to and informative for potential new employees.

Include a 'career' or 'jobs' page in your website that allows anyone who may be interested in working with you to access job descriptions, benefits, salaries or hourly rates or pay, plus any perks that may be unique to your organization. Make sure that interested applicants can upload their resumes to your site vis-a-vis this page.

We're in the 21st century so make sure your site is easily accessible to anyone and everyone with a smartphone. You might even consider creating an 'App' applicants can use to read job posts and file applications for the jobs of their choice.

Your website should help would-be applicants begin to feel comfortable with your organization by including photos and background information on owners, principles, partners, senior managers, supervisors, and other key personnel along with a pictorial essay of how work flows through your facilities.

Some applicants will vet you long before you vet them

Serious applicants will vet your organization in several ways.

They will ask colleagues and friends what they know about your organization, and they'll undoubtedly check out your website and read your blog posts and scroll through social media sites to gain some insight into who you are, where you are, and what you do.

They may even do internet searches on your management team to gain even more profound insights into the character and quality of the women and men who run your organization.

These will be your best candidates . . . the ones who are motivated to do due diligence before they decide that your organization would be an ideal place to work . . . or not.

Present a comprehensive job description

It is important to present a top-notch job description that highlights your organization's mission, values, and vision for the following reasons:

1. You want to attract the best prospective applicants
2. You want to give potential applicants compelling reasons to want to apply

3. You want applicants to understand the job's responsibilities to help them make an informed decision to apply or not

4. You want applicants to take the first step to become committed to your organization

5. Before you invest time and money in the interview process, you want to make sure candidates are likely to fit in with your organization's culture and are capable of making a positive impact on productivity

You might even consider taking the creative step of producing a recruiting video that gives prospective applicants insights into what it would be like to work in your organization.

You can make it simple by filming your employees at work and asking them to talk freely (non-scripted) about how they feel about the organization's culture, values, and mission.

How to attract the right person for the right job

First and foremost, everyone involved in the organization's hiring process should thoroughly understand the job description before any job is posted.

Remember, there are two sides to each job posting: One . . . how the successful candidate will be required to meet the organization's requirements and responsibilities and, two . . . how the organization will reward the successful candidate (salary, benefits, opportunities for advancement, etc.) for his or her ability to meet or exceed the organization's requirements and responsibilities.

If you invest the time and energy it takes to write a clear and concise job description spelling out precisely what the organization wants and what it is willing to give for what it wants, you will attract more qualified, motivated candidates . . . period.

By the way, on whether to include a salary range in a job posting, be smart! Many employers say that when they post jobs without any indication of salary, they receive about one-third fewer applications.

So, don't hesitate to be upfront about compensation. After all, if you're honest with applicants, they'll be more likely to be honest with you.

The Interview – The end all and be all of the hiring process

Common Sense HR Solutions

DavyZ Jones

The interview – the end all and be all of the hiring process

According to a Leadership IQ survey of twenty thousand employees, nearly half failed in the first eighteen months on the job . . . not because they couldn't perform technical tasks but because their attitudes conflicted with their ability to fit into the employer's culture.

You can't afford to lose nearly half the people you hire, so, when you take the final step in the hiring process . . . the interview . . . you'll want to make sure that you:

While it is of course essential to make sure a candidate is technically competent to do the job, we don't necessarily recommend that your interview questions are as extensive as you'd find in the so-called Edison Test.

It is just as important to assess the candidate's soft skills . . . her ability to handle challenging social situations (big egos, negative personalities, etc.) that will enable her to work with a variety of figures, especially during stressful times.

Look for primary clues to help you determine that the candidate's personality fits the job for which she has applied. For example, a candidate with an empathetic character is more suited to be hired as a counselor than as a computer programmer

Ask the right questions for the right reasons

No matter how much (or little) experience you have as an interviewer, you know that you are about to take the final step in determining whether a candidate will be worth the investment the organization will have to make.

As we've already said, you must be able to ask the right questions for the right reasons.

For example, you'll want to ask questions like:

- **Who are you?** – This is an open-ended question that will either rattle your candidate or make her feel at ease. After all, most people love to talk about themselves, and while that's happening, you'll have the opportunity to see for yourself how confident she is and how well she can communicate

- **Tell me about the most challenging situation you ever faced on a job and how you handled it** – The candidate's response will tell you a lot about her honesty, about her fit in the prior employer's culture, and, moreover, about her problem-solving skills

- **How would your colleagues on your current (or prior) job describe you?** – You're asking about the candidate's honesty, strengths and weaknesses, and her ability to get along with others in the workplace

- **Who do you want to be when you're part of a team?** – The answer here will help you confirm the validity of the candidate's response to the prior question and will also give you some insight into her willingness and ability to take responsibility for completing a task to be integrated into the overall effort of the entire team
- **Which of all the projects you worked on for your current (or prior) employer was your favorite and why?** – The response to this question gives you more background information on the candidate's capabilities than you could glean from the candidate's resume.
- **Where will you be in five years?** – The candidate's response will tell you about her objectivity, her commitment to her future, about her overall motivation, and whether she will be likely to remain with your organization.
- **What questions do you have for me?** – You never want to give a candidate a chance to provide you with a 'yes' or 'no' answer by asking "Do you have any questions for me?" It is reasonable to assume that the candidate cares enough about the job she's applied for and has enough respect for your investment in the hiring process to be prepared for this moment. Her response will very likely let you know whether or not to continue your investment in this particular candidate.

Note: The essential responsibility an interviewer has is her willingness to listen. You know as well as anyone that job candidates typically give out more than enough information to help you make the right decision to hir or not.

But if you haven't listened, carefully, objectively, and consistently, to everything the candidate has revealed about herself, you won't be able to check for inconsistencies . . . or consistencies . . . and link back and forth to critical answers that could determine the candidate's ability to succeed or fail in the long-term.

And that . . . success or failure . . . is the name of the game, isn't it?

"We must be the change we wish to see in the world."

~ Mahatma Gandhi

Common Sense HR Solutions

DavyZ Jones

Chapter Contents

Diversity and inclusion is not only about the law — 91

Challenges to diversity and inclusion in the workplace — 94

Proven strategies to promote diversity and inclusion in the workplace — 96

Awareness of unique cultural differences — 99

Points to ponder — 102

Summary — 104

References — 105

Diversity and inclusion is not only about the law

Diversity and inclusion is primarily about understanding, acceptance, and respect between people of various cultures in the workplace.

The U.S. Census Bureau projects that by 2050 more than half of America's workforce will be women and men of color, nearly half of our workforce will be women, and one in five in the workforce will be over 55.

Increasing demographic diversity is an ongoing reality that makes diversity and inclusion strategies imperatives for any organization that expects to survive and thrive in the 21st century.

Technological advances and the growing global economy bring different cultures, unique perspectives, and diverse attitudes, skills, and talents closer together in the workplace than ever before in history.

Rapidly changing demographics affect every manager, supervisor, employee, customer, and competitor and every organization and, as a natural consequence, the overall economy.

If an organization wants to put itself on the path to consistent success in today's global economy, it must recognize that diversity can be a resource, and that inclusion contributes to sustaining a competitive advantage.

What is diversity?

Diversity describes the differences and similarities of individuals in the workplace, including age, ethnicity, gender, physical abilities, political beliefs, race, religious beliefs, sexual orientation, and socio-economic status.

What is inclusion?

Inclusion is the creation of a workplace in which every individual is treated fairly, respectfully, and is wholeheartedly encouraged to use his or her unique abilities, skills, and talents to ensure the organization's success.

Why is it so important to embrace diversity and inclusion?

Diversity is, after all, a resource that is undeniably rich with potential and therefore presents each member of the organization's team with opportunities to expand his or her outlook on diversity and inclusion while utilizing creative strategies to pursue consistent success.

For an organization to consistently achieve meaningful productivity and profit goals while maintaining a competitive advantage, owners, managers, and all employees must be willing to invest in the firm's single greatest resource: the diverse abilities, skills, and talents of every person in the workforce.

Challenges to Diversity and Inclusion in the Workplace

Challenges to diversity and inclusion in the workplace

Implementing viable diversity and inclusion policies in the workplace is challenging, and some of those challenges include:

Communication – Cultural, perceptual, and language obstacles must be overcome for diversity and inclusion policies to work in any organization. Failure to adequately communicate diversity and inclusion policies can result in misperceptions, low employee morale, and the subsequent lack of teamwork.

The difficulty of integrating diversity and inclusion workplace policies – Management must design, develop, and implement customized diversity and inclusion policies to suit the unique needs of the organization's workforce.

Diversity training – One-time diversity training is not sufficient to sustain diversity and inclusion policies for the long-term. Recurring diversity training will work to reinforce and maintain a company-wide diversity and inclusion culture that permeates every department.

Hesitance to fully adapt – There will be some employees who will maintain a 'we've always done it this way' attitude and will hesitate to fully adapt to accept cultural and social change in the workplace.

Common Sense HR Solutions *DavyZ Jones*

Proven strategies to promote diversity and inclusion

Proven strategies to promote diversity and inclusion

Build interpersonal relationships – Employees can help promote diversity and inclusion while improving productivity by learning about the beliefs, histories, interests, and lives of their colleagues.

Defeat resistance with inclusion – A proven strategy to defeat opposition to diversity and inclusion policies involves encouraging every employee to help in the formulation and execution of those policies in the workplace.

Diversity assessment – An objective assessment and evaluation of diversity and inclusion needs is the obvious first step in designing policies that will achieve the organization's long-term productivity and profitability goals. An employee diversity survey will go a long way to helping management define challenges and obstacles unique to the organization's workplace.

Diversity plan implementation – Owners and managers must make public and personal commitments to diversity and inclusion in the workplace by incorporating appropriate policies into every aspect of the organization's internal and external business processes.

Honor culturally significant holidays – Management can acknowledge all faiths present in the organization's workplace and offer paid-time off for employees to celebrate cultural events and holidays, including Gay Pride celebrations and the International Day of Persons with Disabilities, the International Day for the Elimination of Racial Discrimination, etc.

Offsite activities – Management can provide opportunities for employees to create, plan for, and interact in off-site activities where individuals and groups can get to know each other as people and begin to find ways to drop barriers to cultural acceptance.

Promote a company-wide attitude of transparency – Inclusion includes encouraging all employees to freely offer their opinions, ideas, and suggestions on how best to facilitate diversity and inclusion in the workplace.

Workplace diversity and inclusion plan – The organization's strategy must be attainable, comprehensive, enforceable, viable, and should include a well-defined milestone chart.

Awareness of unique cultural differences

Awareness of unique cultural differences

It is essential for management, key personnel, and employees to be aware of and understand some of the individual cultural differences that may exist in the workplace, including but not limited to:

Community needs versus self-needs - In some cultures, people make extra efforts to make sure the community's needs take precedence while in other cultures, people are more focused on self-interest.

Conflict resolution - In some cultures, people prefer to deal with conflict quickly and directly while in other cultures, people tend to avoid confrontation to maintain individual and group dignity.

Conversational breaks of silence - In some cultures, it is perfectly acceptable for one person to be silent for extended periods of time during a conversation. In other cultures, people engage in ongoing dialogues and may even feel comfortable making 'small talk.'

Personal space and physical contact - In some cultures, people are not inhibited about physical contact and may not refrain from engaging in displays of physical contact. In other cultures, people are expected to be cautious about physical contact and may not even think it appropriate to shake hands with a member of the opposite sex.

Time – Various cultures measure time differently. Some cultures measure time more rigidly and are more time-oriented while other cultures are more time-flexible and casual.

Common Sense HR Solutions

DavyZ Jones

Points to ponder

Points to ponder

- An organization that honors, develops, and sustains a diverse workplace, attracts and retains committed, productive employees while increasing and maintaining vendor and customer loyalty.
- Diversity is not just a legal consideration; diversity is a proven resource that improves workplace harmony, increases productivity, adds to the bottom line, and promotes a competitive advantage.
- Diversity is unfortunately often viewed primarily as an issue of disability, ethnicity, gender, and/or race linked to local, state, and federal protection laws and regulations.
- Diversity should be an essential component in any organization's HR policy manual and should include a variety of initiatives to meet the variable needs of management, employees, customers, and vendors.
- Employee 'buy-in' and consistent support for the organization's diversity and inclusion policies is essential to its ability to increase productivity and consistently promote customer and vendor loyalty.
- Owners, managers, and key personnel must take the ultimate responsibility for the development and application of viable diversity and inclusion policies and must, therefore, incorporate those policies into every aspect of the organization's mission.

Common Sense HR Solutions

Davy2 Jones

Summary

Summary

Viable diversity and inclusion policies will evolve from a strategic plan that incorporates the organization's baselines, benchmarks, metrics, and tactical outreach and recruiting efforts designed to increase workplace diversity.

The organization's advancement and promotional paths should be transparent to increase and sustain numbers of diverse employees in management roles.

Diversity and inclusion is not the same as antidiscrimination because anti-discrimination is a legal term that requires employers to meet the minimum requirements of local, state, and federal laws and regulations. As we've said, diversity and inclusion is not about the law . . . it is about understanding, acceptance, and respect between people of various cultures in the workplace.

Interactive diversity training, mentoring, and employee resource groups are essential components of any functional diversity and inclusion initiative.

The business case for developing a viable diversity and inclusion policy involves designing and implementing strategies that help management and employees fully comprehend how to monitor and manage diversity and inclusion to create a harmonious, profitable workplace.

References

References

A Matter of Difference – By B. M. Ferdman and M. N. Davidson in *The Industrial-Organizational Psychologist*, 2001 to 2004, focusing on diversity and inclusion)

All Charges Alleging Harassment (FY 2010-FY 2015) - U.S. Equal Employment Opportunity Commission, *Enforcement & Litigation Statistics*, U.S. Equal Employment Opportunity Commission, *Annual Reports on the Federal Work Force (Part I)*, *EEO Complaint Processing, Fiscal Years 2010-2015*

All Charges Alleging Harassment (FY 2010-FY 2015) - U.S. Equal Employment Opportunity Commission, *Enforcement & Litigation Statistics*, U.S. Equal Employment Opportunity Commission

An Examination of the Nature and Correlates of Ethnic Harassment Experiences - Kimberly T. Schneider et al., J. Applied Psychol. 3 (2000).

Creating and Sustaining Diversity and Inclusion in Organizations: Strategies and Approaches. By E. Holvino, B. M. Ferdman, & D. Merrill-Sands (2004). In P. Stockdale & F. Crosby (Eds.),

Creating the Multicultural Organization: A Strategy for Capturing the Power of Diversity - By T. Cox, Jr. (2001). San Francisco: Jossey-Bass.

Dancing with Resistance: Leadership Challenges in Fostering a Culture of Inclusion. By I. Wasserman, P. V. Gallegos & B. M. Ferdman (in press) - In K. M. Thomas (Ed.), Mahwah, NJ:

Developing Competency to Manage Diversity: Readings, Cases & Activities - By T. Cox, Jr. & R. L. Beale. (1997). San Francisco: Berrett-Koehler.

Employee and Employer Characteristics Associated with Elevated Risk of Filing Disability Harassment Charges, 36 - Linda Shaw et al., J. Vocational Rehab.187 (2012).

Gender harassment: Broadening Our Understanding of Sex-Based Harassment at Work - Emily A. Leskinen et al., 35 Law and Human Behavior 25 (2011)

Important Factors to Consider When Using Internal Branding as a Management Strategy: A Healthcare Case Study - Rodney Peter Gapp & Bill Merrilees, 14 J. Brand Mgmt. 162 (2006).

It's Unfair: Why Customers Who Merely Observe an Uncivil Employee Abandon the Company, Christine Porath et al., J. Serv. Res. 1 (2011); Christine Porath et al., **AARP Bulletin Poll on Workers 50+:** Dawn Nelson,

AARP, *Executive Summary*

Making Differences Matter: A New Paradigm for Managing Diversity - By D. A. Thomas &. R. J. Ely. (*Harvard Business Review*, 1996, September-October).

Managing Diversity: The Courage to Lead - By E. Y. Cross. (2000). Westport, CT: Quorum.

Managing Diversity: Toward a Globally Inclusive Workplace. By M. E. Mor Barak. (2005). Thousand Oaks, CA: Sage Publications.

Racial and Ethnic Harassment in the Workplace in Gender, Race, and Ethnicity in the Workplace: Issues and Challenges for Today's Organizations - Tamara A. Bruce, (Margaret Foegen Karsten, ed., 2006).

Report on the Status of People with Disabilities: A Survey of Faculty and Staff at the University of New Hampshire - Jennifer Vanderminden & Carol Swiech, Fall2011.

The Experience of Bystanders of Workplace Ethnic Harassment - K.S. Douglas Low *et al.*, 37 J. Applied Social Psychol. 2261 (2007).

The Inclusion Breakthrough. By F. A. Miller & J. H. Katz. (1995). San Francisco: Berrett-Koehler.

The Power of Inclusion. By M. C. Hyter & J. L. Turnock. (2005). Mississauga, Ontario: Wiley.

www.ingramcontent.com/pod-product-compliance
Lightning Source LLC
Chambersburg PA
CBHW071653240526
45469CB00021B/2270